Words In Memory
SERGE GAVRONSKY

SPUYTEN DUYVIL
New York City

Library of Congress Cataloging-in-Publication Data

Names: Gavronsky, Serge, author.
Title: Words in memory / Serge Gavronsky.
Description: New York City : Spuyten Duyvil, [2022]
Identifiers: LCCN 2022023171 | ISBN 9781956005769 (paperback)
Subjects: LCGFT: Poetry.
Classification: LCC PS3557.A957 W67 2022 | DDC 811/.54--dc23/
eng/20220518
LC record available at https://lccn.loc.gov/2022023171

Doctor

An autumnal calm
A Nurse pops in
Ok! Today! Which arm?
"As you like it!"
She thinks once again
And thinks into his arm
Was that painful?
Much ado about nothing
And adds:
Your bike friends
Left you as an invalid!
When will my quarantine
End?
Much ado about nothing
She mutters to herself

In a near distance
Flags sway
Sea winds crush sea winds
See winds shuffle

O!—lieutenant, where have all of them gone?
Titles remain for the time being
Titles unfurl
Images
A feather remains in flight
A missed conversation
When A voice interrupts
When will my quarantine
End when Eyes cloud words
A bunch of Clouds

A lieutenant says: "give me a drink"
A cloud
Slumbers
Bikes need oil
In someone's eyes
Hell's a coming
A bike becomes a
Motorcycle   When it gives
a sign

                                    Nobody can
read

What a

Pleasure he says

Winds

A tree

A road

Wounds

As a rider sweeps the road

When the bicycle crashed

Out of books

Fell

On the razors

Edge

Time keeping time

All my buddies

Nearly dead

   The Bhagavad Gita

   Muktananda

   The Thirteen Principal Upanishads

         Wheel

A round

He rose

Cleaned his biography wished there
A need to Underline
He fell on top of his bike
And then his poetry--
A sidelined reality
Pushing his mind
Into another word
I look at the road
Why then
EYES
Asked myself on paper

Why ask myself as if
Eyes were another
Being
Until
Eyes distant

Eyes
Know what's best

Then I   But then
Knew

Flat on my
Remembrances
I muttered
No relation to Happiness

He tried to lift the left wheel
Off his leg

Then he
Quoted what always
Rode in front of his
One of his wheels

Wheels
Below the Thirteen Principal
Upanishads

What memories flight
Rides
The skirt
A white nurse' s uniform
For action

On a

Sheer road

Lying on
My

Leather bound
My body
Cleanses
Distant sirens

          A road

Holding
My dreams
Now
I hear them

My voice scratched
Words in my head

          Please, Sir

Would you

             Please

So I can clean
Your   wounds

             She

In her
White
Uniform
A white
Uniform worn
White then she threw
A white feather on my body
I whispered to my thoughts
Into her
White lining

Her breasts.
"He is here, somewhere between her nipples"
Catullus

But the poet is clearer in my thoughts

                    Take off Your clothes,
 I said

Your clothes (I said) quickly, while
Your beauty is attainable

                    Put them on the chair

I said then, in a fury, for which I am still ashamed
You smell as though you needed a bath. Take off
your clothes and
Purify
Yourself
Self

She shifted
My thoughts then
I remembered before
I crashed
I imagined   A line

Left

In Shiva's line

    I.   Whispered to the pillow

    II.   The body

Speaking
I shall now
Place
My left leg
Dropped
Under my left leg
My left leg

That's why My Body
Scales wisdom
For I am the body of this earth

Sleep
She

She said as a team
Of white

Doctors
Uniforms circling my
Body
Hands
Fingers
Blighting white

                              As if when
                              Wheels turn

I thought

'They might
No
I said to myself
Later
Feed him light
Food
Water
A poem or two
I dreamed of my
Rebirth
On a white road

Surrounded
By dead leaves

Then I rebirthed
As an animal
Why should I not
Rebirth

Then I THOUGHT OF A
REBIRTH
In her hands
Why be
Impartial
Or was it all
A comedy of
Desires
The mind is a Roman
Parent
These
I DON'T NEED TO TELL
YOU EVERYTHING

ALL

THINGS
GYRATE IN MY HEAD

Wheels swerving
A tree branch
Across
A road alone
That round
Will never
Forget me
In my leather
Outfit

Please do not
Tell me everything
Even if I drawl out the
Truth

She pushed my
Pillow
UNDER
My
Dreams

Could ALL of them
Dream all
Of …
I didn't know what happened
Next

                    Lights out
She stumbled away
Holding my book

Difficult to read

Difficult to tell what
A pile of rubber

Moves a branch
Happened in the garden
Not even

A branch
Below my
Window

Shiva

Then out of a quieter mouth
He recited a line
From
Racine

But then he energetically
Said out of his knowledge
My happiness bears hardly any
Relationship to happiness
Or
To reality
Doctor
You've not had your dinner
Close by

From the next bed
The doc hears
And remembers
A line out of Moliere's
L'Etourdi

"La fin d'une vraie et pure comedie"

A nurse barges in and says

Doctor, maybe he never went to college!

OK! There's another line:

"The Wheel of Earth"

Gt!

Ok! I let you know About Shiva

"Listen, listen, it comes from the Wheel of Death

          Death as a Rebirth

How about a line from Moliere's Etourdi

Mascarille says:

          "La fin d'une vraie et pure comedie"

Doctor, he does not know any Foreign language!

Dear White dress! Your cherished white ass!

I then thought

Of another poet's lines

  "But you!

—In your white lace dress

The dying swan

You're the most college graduate, working the night
shift! Where did

you ever get your college degree?

I also remembered one of my friend's poem's line

The bodies are clean and white
—Arm, leg
The body is clean
And white

Well, You know the fountain? You know across Broad-
way, all you've got to do is open your eyes!! That's
where I did my undergraduate work as a...you'll never
guess it, as a French major, and I got a prize for speak-
ing, writing and praises for my memory, especially a
text I really loved!"

"Could it have been "Speaking of Shiva?"
You're on the right track, well, if you want the whole
truth, when I went to college, our teacher knew Shake-
speare and especially his love texts... And he would
always add Michael McClure's STAR poems!"
Doctor, have you ever..."

As a matter of poetry, he could quote the first
line and here goes! "

THE PLUMES OF LOVE

I said to myself, in my own trans-
lation, my own translation in French, my own
translation out of that SEXY

Bhagavad Gita

Doc I've got his
Done
Doc
Me too
His afternoon
Stops

Where are you, doc!!!

Here
Above your
Chinese signs
Doctor where are
YOU Yes, YOU
Waiting
I've got
His daily
Thermometer

 Nurse says: "Why?"
A branch stakes

Its truth
His functions

Nurse replies
"Why go?"

Why I'm waiting for his
O shit!
Still Waiting
Nurse interrupts:

I got his...
His food tray
Doc Please

I'm here
I'm here
Here!
Nurse replies
Where's here?
Waiting for him
Doc he'll come
Waiting
For what
You ask
The proper question
He says listen

Says the
The nurse
Says truthfully
2nd edition
What she says:
The House of cards!

I say, Doc what's he saying?

An Introduction

All

He says with a silent

Man's drawl

Nurse

My favorite nurse

When will my

Quarantine end?

Unity

The Hindu Religious tradition

OK!

OK!

Let me add

The Why of

Torah

Doc! How did

You

Guess?

All my bike

Buddies

Where have they all gone
I gave it a minus thought
And then
I said it must have
Been
Then I asked my nurse

When will my quarantine end?
When will my quarantine end?
Isn't it always the same question
I went to my graduate exams
Hoped
You
Made
It?

Glad you
Asked?
Nurse, please go
On your rounds?

Under a theater
The Hindu
The Chinese second edition

Edition

How I would like to dominate

That

Experience

Nurse, put the food tray on his left

Next to the Figaro

I'd love, says the nurse

Read French or

Some language from D!

Stop! Stop! Stop!

Says the doctor

The nurse adds

The Life of Torah

I've heard all of that before

Check his bowl

I know: Movements

Put the tray under his

Bed!

That's all?

Ok! Here's my

Last…

The Life of Torah!
I remember as he dropped his…
The doctor says:

Well,
I've
For…
Forgetting!
Doc! Please your
Hand
From
My insides! (she laughs)
Then, she added:
"Oh
Doc!"
Let me read a line from
Buddhism! If I may
That China and Japan, Buddhist Tradition and…Doc
Watch that beer before it tips. Doctor
Check his bowel movements! He's chewing!
Nurse, would you
pull your white
Blouse a little
Further down

In the mean time
Up and away! Up!
Nothing better
He says to her white
His nurse
Check out

The religious Life of Man
Enough is gut enough
Then all's
For me
Doc says to his
Nurse
All's well when
It's well he laughs
He

Says she is a comin!

Nurse, admire his bowel movement!
Doc says in edition!

Read this:

The Second Part of King James

The Third
The
Third
Part of
Titus Andronicus
Oxford U Press
London New York Toronto
And... Lyons?
A true chef and then a few
Triadic titles including
Timothy of Athens
Nurse would you be
Kind
Enough to pull the shade
UP
I'm only a graduate student
As far as I'm concerned

Nurse says in perfect English
"Fine! Fine"
I Find and then
How many more
How
And
The
Prince of
Wales

West End
Avenue close to a food
Store

Here, take my
Handkerchief and
Wipe your
Nose
Two lives or was it
A Dead pan!
Hear that panting Glass whistle
                              I'll never
Tell

Hey Nursy! Put the tray
On his table

Something
Sorry! I say, Sorry!
Call an attendant!
Why?
My why
Is
Enough

                              ADD

p. 260
Nurse, I did first wallow in his
Urine, dribble down his
Left
Side! left side
Lights dim
Hey Doc! Lights
Dim!
I'll wait in
The cafeteria downstairs
Listen-in to talking Doc who says

Fuck them all up on all tables on all floors I've got

An

Appointment in the

Cafeteria

                            I said

Looking

Around the

Merry

Wives of Jersey

                                  Wrong

Ok!

The third Part of Henry James

Nurse finishes

                        Titus

How's that reply

Or

In

The

Plural!

Or

India, China and…Japan!

Then,

He

Turns on in his
Memory and
Says
Celie, Laila

                    And

Any
Other Words?
Try out

                    any page (Any…) ANY

 Mon Coeur avait raison

              She wipes

Her left hand
She, too, as if her finger
Thought of pleasure

Says to
Herself
"Hey Doc!"

              Doc had already

Left
All that's a
Tragedy of Errors!
I'll see your clever body

In his
Breath the smell
Nurse where are you
Going?
Nurse smiles

Wash my left hand
Wash

My nose
Under her breath she says:
Lead me on

Bella Nurse this is bed 25.
He's bed 26 and thus
When he makes a steady snorting music, he keeps me
In another Language scape.
Come,
Please, otherwise, what's to become of my sleep?
"I'll come right always!
Here's
My arm
So   Come,

I'm here.

Please nurse shoot my thigh

I too would love to dose him a straight shot

I Agreeeee! Please,

You too can hear his plaints!

Nurse prepares a needle.

She says: "Move over! Use your towel, and lift up

Your

Off

A shot.

Hear him!

The elevator stops

Nurse makes it to that open door!

In your absence, let me quote

Music and then...Music,

Again and again

Please,

Chew off your quotes! Whose voice is so pro-
nounced

I've got to leave you for my elevator is right here!
It makes her come…

Got it?

Got it
Yes just a pound of it!
Yes

I can hear the elevator crunching
Time
This is bed 25
Where… I'm waiting for 26
Sounds of an elevator door closing
I Got my needle

I'll be right there, Number 26!

 Number D smiles and says:
"All's well that shall begin well"
So, well! Ok!

Roll up your arm

Think
Of two French naked women,
Painted by:
Seurat ...
Or was it some other like Picasso??

Then the other bikes flew by
Think of two
And close your eyes.
Lick your hands   Where is the
impossible

Sounds of a late elevator
Please...Please come back and pull up my sheets,
as far as

They can go!
See you with your breakfast!
Now, he dreams as far as she can come   back
Now   he hears the service elevator
See you with breakfast!
Ever hear

                    "Make my day! "

You make my 24 hours pass!

I hear the elevator door opening

He rolls over,
Lifts his bed sheet.
Whispers to himself

Oh! How I'd like to eat her up!

Bed 26 whispers:
Could I share
Your Dreams?

Mine alone!

I dream of her
Body and her ass
Dreams define reality
Like mine.
Ready   for the night

Injection
Do not touch me!
She aims the needle
She says: Please, don't move

He says
Was the tea
Hot enough.?

Please
Give bed 26 his shot!

He says

Nurse's elevator
Voices! Let's go
He'll survive
You can hear the elevator purring
Descend
Ground floor says,
In a recorded voice:
When you lean into me, I can read your
name dream: when you lean

Into me, roll up my sleeve and...you lean and...your
breasts touch my
Chin.

NOW
My memory rests on names I gave you:
Mistress Page.
You as a servant

Remember
"Hush Hush"
And if I can
Remember

Cressida
Juliet
Lady Macbeth
Lucrecius
Venus
Cheops

Gertrude
O miracle of men

Let me touch you
Guess!
With names,
Add Ophelia in the water
You will Never guess my name
A hello speaks

Too soon
O those fine women!
All turn to the right
Turn to the right, brush up with your right
hand

My right hand?

As quiet as a front line!

                              Hear a

side of

                              Words

You
Are
My

Angel of pleasures!

Now

Lights off

Please, turn off your dream!

I.   Always smile

II.   You're so close

III.   To my left arm

IV.   Soon my quiet muffles myself

V.   Again! Once again, my left shoulder,

My sleep will seize itself

Then by other names

As if I had a half dozen sleep

I must go, needles and all!

Sleep well

See your arm in the

Early morning.

You know, I have to go my rounds

Can you please move your hand!

Lots of seconds   Rust

Words

I'll dream
Of you!

I hear

Steps!

I say to you
Never turn off
The lights
I dream of you
A bushel of words

My mother used to say
Please, watch out for your grammar!
Yell!
If you need to!
Nurse, hear me ring my bell
Even if it's a
Dream!

> When I sleep
> Another turn of
> Wheels

Please
Never   more take my pulse!
Keep your schedule

Smile as if I had
Collected all your thoughts
Standing there by
The elevator
I hope you'll always
Go down

Downstairs
Waits for you
By the way
Are you alone
In your head
Alone alone?

A voice next to mine?

Keep your fantasies

Move

Your body

Clean and white

Your

Body

White!   All to yourself

In the morning, according to my body's desires

Let me dream a

Dream

Further on

I yell

Your body. Follows a

Schedule

Please Push up my pillow

I scream for my

Nurse

My nurse

Where

All are you?

Pull the shower curtain
I dream
Feel your left hand
Me me me
Yells bed 26

Come
Lean against me your
Needle

All is a deadly
Quiet

Bed 26
yells
Birds have left
Their trees
My wheels
All is as

Quiet as her will
My bike on its side

Read if you're about
To die   A fog follows my
Listen   Clutter of desires

Your jargon eats super!
Writes Moliere
Waits in the middle
Of day's time

                                 Let let it be

Now it's daylight
Provided you
Take the Broadway
Bus
I should have skipped that
Memory
Clean

In front of a book
San Gimignano

I throw a
Wish
A heavy

Tray

Wheels keep on turning
An example of Madness
Wheels
A life   Holds down lines
Spells itself

                                              Only a
                                              Spirit
                                              Holds

The truth

Why why
Thirteen
Holds time?

He's talking
To a unicorn

Goats are

Skin and
Empty of
Words
When wheels stutter
By a tree

Down
Here
Thoughts
Refuse to read
Thirteen principal editions
Dream white body
Edition as if time were
A threshold
She is a dream escaped
Comes with her needle
Closer and closer
Dreaming a tiny pain

Page after
Page

A nurse's body
White
Duration below
A bed
Sliding
An escape blinds
Those who refuse to go

A long signal
A Cosmological
Desire

                    A Timelessness of sounds

On a road
Wheels motionless
Lost time
A branch

Always
A branch

Above
A skeleton dreams
Perched over
A nurse well read
Always
An imaginary
Eye

Rebirth
White
Uniform
Quiet
As
A wheel

Torching

Pages after
Pages

Of desires

The name of a
Mountain
Far above
Waiting
For my body
Clean and
Leather Bound

How else to
Spell words
Thoughts
As if
They were
Always
Hiding

Eyes looking
Blank
Double link
Turning wheels

Sometimes
Ugly tires
Lost
A narrative
Solitary words
A side

                              Here
                              Always

Backward time
Lost

Did he sing
Did he cry
Did he yell

He breathed

The softness of skin
In black leather
Breathing
A break in time

A kindness

Cannot spell

Forgotten
Now how to
Spell
As if spelling made
Human
Time pass

A voyage to
Silence

Hear a pulse
A cosmological
YES or NO

Suddenly
As if I had
Invented time

And

Made
A
Gesture
Just to
Move my Words

She smiles a letter
Counts a leather elbow

Bed
26
Yells out his language
How close he says death
Seems to
Me

After a loud dream
The elevator

Murmurs
Steps in white
Please
Take this tray

A wait but I've
Got to scream
My hands tied
A sheet
Falls

Only ideas
Cover
Steps
The noise
Of the elevator

Nothing harms
The silence
As if in black leather jackets

Already in
Bed
Straightens out
His thoughts

Where

Is the place for
Dreams
When her white
Sneakers avoid
Noise

The end fails to sleep
Darkness rumbles

Why 13 steps
She asks
Why?
The Upanishad
Thinking words
Throw them
Into oblivion

Dreams the
Andes in
Translation
In many ways
Always
A silent return

When dreams
Walk
Out sliding

Silent as an absence
Footsteps

Nothing
Left
It
A flat silence
Dark

But then
I try to invent
What's next and so
On and
So as a manner of voice
Speech voided

                        Give meaning to

Chance
By Darkness

Purge words
But it must be
A Castle of invisible words

Painted
As a specter of
Image-words

And without
A Word-breath
Words in
Echoes
Conclude
Words
Each recognizes
Itself where
Words disappeared
In thought
Grown
In a cycle
Almost there
Walking corridors
Muffle

Her white words
My word
Her wishes
Then Night falls

Meaning
Words
Hold out to desire
Once said
Words disappear
Written in breath

Slide your arm
Out of your sheets
Whitened desires
The sound of heels
A voice
She will come
Tied to words

A horse becomes
Itself a line

You heard
What you think
When you hear yourself

Trophies
Clean your hands
In a nighttime
Summer's dream
Playfully
Cluttered

On a blank
Dreams swallowed
Beyond themselves
In a swallowed word
Hers
She singles out
Then
Stuck
Without a breath of

Words, then

More words
Crying.
Dreams caught fire Breathing
So close

Burning
Themselves
Your pulse
In silence
Footsteps in a corridor
Ears plugged
He whispers the Globe blocks
In shattered friendships
Myself on the 11th floor

She then says I'm going

But who would ever have thought

The price of Corn Flakes

Now

Guessing all's well

In words
Near an elsewhere with
Friends
Or
Diamonds on his wrist
Anybody
Others would say
Faster with a blade
Imagined

It hurts
Do not
Tell my other
Why secrets
Cloud a bike
Say, what's the meaning now?
But what's a meaning?

It hurts

The doctor says
I'll be back
Even if you're asleep I'll be
Back, I swear, he smiles.
I'll be back.
Take my word for it, or for that
Scene
He speaks
Fears
But muted
In a whisper
He mumbles
Let that needle prick me!

There's an elephant
Game of
Chance
Mumbles
Now another pleasure

He yells out
I wrote Tractatus

There's always a game
Of chance
Nurse says he whispered
Tractatus

Days go
Nights go faster now
Go faster, now
Hear him whisper
Tractatus
Gorgeous, he thinks

Doc
Please
Another needle prick

Bed number 24
Mumbles

A repetition
A pin
Please, your pin prick!

"Nurse, what's he saying
Always the same
He yells
Tractatus

How fast
Days go
Boundlessly
By
I wrote that, and after a
Double
Speak of Shiva,

She waits
Hums
Checks out her uniform
Bed number 24
Thinks out loud
Gorgeous!
He repeats
"Wittgenstein"

In German like one of

His German professors

Love's Labor Lost.

You look Gorgeous!

You look great!

You just broke silence!

Please

By the way why is he here?

Knocked down by a singing   BIKE

On the ground, he says

Elsewhere

Cars hit him

Nobody's there

She says Dinner

Is rolling in

Let me push you down

Whatever you

Want please

Lean into my tray

Its good

For you

Now

We'll drive
Toward the elevator doors!
How stunning your movements!

　　　He thinks
You're

A dreamscape

Always waiting
Where are my brothers?
How can I ever forget my
Brothers?
My rich friends in Vienna
I'll never forget
That collector
Of netsuke
So rich living in
A chateau next to my home
I can still see them
Worked in porcelain
I told you for my dinner
No string beans! Ok

She says
I'll prick the next bed
I'll eat mashed potatoes he'll…
Ok! I'll give it to the next one
bed 34 as she sways
"I'll wheel you
"Hey Doc, don't forget me
I love your pencil!!
Love those wheels to
The down elevator
In front of the elevators
The down elevator

Her nurse's uniform
The way her body swings
As she wheels me there
Then
He says, staring at her
White uniform

"Love's labor lost…"
Thinks 24

Hear my dreams!
I hear dogs growling

Dogs duplicate
Spill over barks
In a storm
I harness
Her footsteps
Where you thunder
As in an Attic painting

All I want
Are dishes
String beans
Words
Cooked to
Perfection!
Like our
small size
Turn around
I want to gaze
At you
You've already

Told me that
Nurse, can you tell me what I smell?
Smells like something
Spells like Memory
Going light in
Berlin Stories. A cover
As in a rainstorm
Plug in the rest
Or travel light
As flakes in the
Night
Dressed for a
Day's dream
He took her
Hand
Swallowed it at day's
Break
He wonders
Tell me what's
That smell?
I smell some thing
Cooking
I see black curtains

Hiding my day!
A time for mists
Or corn flakes
What's
In a name
when origins
Spurt out the truth
In a shadow
I see a tree trunk
All in my Head
You're my
Favorite nurse

The smell of
A good farewell? Think
Of an elevator door
Closing

Elevator doors empty
A flip of a coin

How blue can
Hell be when you're
With me

I smell perfume
A teasing man's mask

Past dreams now a dream
Dreamscape
Words designate

Desires
They Speak a language
Nobody can spell

Books, downstairs
Pages waiting

I want to get out
The shadow's
Shadow
I see it every day

A bike
Then

There's always a
Diction
But who can
Spell
I see a black
Cloud rising
From below
Don't take it
Seriously
Listen to the bed
Next to silence
Yours
Soon he'll be
Gone
"You are
Therefore
I am"

Once a phrase
Doubles

A significant
Sign of a
Sign?
Then, it's thrown away
And when a dream awakes pain

As in a space where
A space conceals her body
Waiting for her midnight walk

In her white sneakers
Working Overtime
Saved

By words

Talk of meaning
Now
I know
I'll remember her
Standing by the elevator

In her white

Speaking
As if in Love
Finally found
Itself out of
The darkness of memory
A touchstone

Dreams
Covered in white sheets
Covers over my dreams
Cast away
I thank my desires
Not having been cast
Away in a Dream

Itself
A musical line
In a toy's mind

Memory
In a sudden recall

Thinks of philosophy
As if in a dream
Slept
Away
A dream
Philosopher's wand
What remained
A repetitive thought
Unwritten

Elastic Darkness

In darkness

         Where front wheels turn

      There's

Always

An End

                              Can it be real

                              A motion
                              Wheels

into

Words rising out of leather

A story
A mind conceals

                              A nurse disappears

Words
Thoughts
Sought
Out
Words

define a void

A letter
Defining itself
Into a void

A silence mistaken
For   meaning
Whipped
Into
Thoughtless meaning

Too
Late as if forgotten
    As if titles failed to remember

        Shuffled meaning

Meanings
As
An
Accident on an open road
Fast as

Words define themselves
Asking where have they all
All slide into new shapes
Only titles remain

A thought in the mouth
Leaves flat on the road

Could it have worked another way?
On top of crushed
Leaves
Banking a possible other
Crushed
Front wheels
Maybe
somebody will remember

Upanishad

Wheels

The thirteenth
Sidelining reality

Eyes

Remember
Words like dusk
Poetry

Other words
For a road
Leaves on the road
A bike flat on a country road
Slides
Slides
You thought what's the weight
Of silence silenced

ANOTHER WAY

She wraps me in a white sheet
Rolls me in my
Staring ahead

She says
What's he's saying

It's all a multiple souvenir
A dream spells out
What she's hearing

Mumbling
Stumbling

I hear above his thoughts
I hear sounds of meaning
What's that
Silence?

OK! Don't
Get ahead of me

We'll soon   Be a
"There"

                              Autumnal
Silence
They still cry out
Hey doc! Don't forget
Me!

Leave
Sounds
In their places
Remain
Where

            You Are where…

I see
Constantly
The same sound
Hear me
Crash
Now
I hear

My throat tries whispering
Whisper words
Above my head
I can see the roof of time
Tell me
What's that
White sounds
All white sounds

In a dream
Both of us
I am your
Nurse, she repeats
Don't
Stare
Stop moving
You
Don't have to
Keep up that horror
That ambulance has its own rites
She says

Tonight

                                        I'll say

Then
I'll ask
You chicken
In bed
She will say
Which arm?

Don't stare

It wont hurt

A pin prick.

Look up at the ceiling

Won't hurt

Which arm

She repeats

I've had lots who

Ask

Which arm

Don't stare at my

Arm, there's little

Of it left

You choose

Left or right

I've done this

A thousand time

Ok!

Lift your

Left leg higher

As you like it

I dream of you

My bike

Should have killed

That tree
Speaking into
It's own

Branches
She laughs
She covers me
For my night
Dreaming

The left one Ok?
He shakes his
Head as if
The immediate past
Had already left him
Body and soul

She snickers
OK
Didn't hurt
I told you
So
I'll be

Back in

2 hours

You'll see me again

Give me

2 hours of a wait

You get

Acquainted

You'll see me again

She says

Every three hours

It's me

I'll open

darkness

Somebody else

The

Same needle

A pin

Smacks

Meaning

Your

Shoulder

She shuffles away
A nurse
He asks her
Where have
All those
Needles gone?

She says in silence
"Fuck up!"

                                I'll be

Back
            She answers
Yours truly,

On a
        silence
 Of a tree
Soundless
As if a
Crash stayed
Silent

You'll
Hear silence
For a
While
That's a
Promise
She snickers
Sees a word
Hears a word
"Where have they all gone?
They must all

                                        have

Gone

 Walked away

In a broken dream
He mutters

I promise
Back on my rounds
For you!
Hear them

Yell

Don't

Bother

It'll be

Alright

Promise

Where have

All gone

A friend says

Says

Don't listen

In a close by

Distance

Bed 26

Where have all gone?

Where

He can hear a repetition

A repetition

One dead

One with a fractured body

They say

Please
Close
The
Window   I hear
birds outside
A night passes by
He pulls up
His white sheet

Your friends
Bikers
Left you
Dead in there
Minds

I said
Pull over we'll
Take care,
Care of
You!

An orchestra of
Loud

Dreams next to mine

By
Winds
Harbor dream

You see
I promised you
I'd
Be back
Please
Stay
Right leg, a sigh
I hear you
I hear them
I hear food trays roll
I feel her hands
I feel my pillow talk
Inside my memory
She can hear flags
Shouting

Once again
Here's
My right leg
Hit me again

Let others yell
A pin prick is all
I'll ever feel
See my thought
Tonight

Where have
All of
Them

                                                    Gone

Gone
Bed 27 or
28
Slides
Back into the aisle
Of minds

Its all a dream

Do you remember

Then

He tries

Please

No shots

No pin prick

                                       Where have all

Words

                                         gone

He vomits

A broom

Next to my

Bed

No doctor hiding behind my curtain

Deal me another dream

The smell of

Food

I'll be back

At six

She checks

Her time

In a near distance
You can hear
Flags flying

Hey
You
Shut your
Fucking
Mouth
Shut
Don't
Talk
She'll be
Back
Fix
Your
Pillows
Your
Crumbled sheets

He can see
Clouds
Slumbering

Branches

A sign
A voice
He tries to free
Himself from
Under
A branch
His black leather jacket
Torn   LATER
His grand-mother
Says
Where's the rest
Your friends
Bikers in the night
A sign
Any sign will do
A crash
He says to himself

Winds blow words

Fallen trees

Tree

                                        Alright as a

Together

                                        Death

A cloud cemetery
Only rocks can talk
Memories
He rumbles
In someone's
Eyes

Only riders

                                        Slumber words

A wound
A pleasure
Sweeping a road
Night falls

Nobody can

Read
Signs

Wounds
Cry out
A repetition
A line out of a margin
What's to remember

Why don't you clean up
Your mind today or else
The mind will do it by   Itself

When will a souvenir awake
Memory without
Wheels

But then
No chance for it

To push memory aside

As on a record
Leave memory
Alone

                                   A matter of

Words

A Memory
But who can
Remember
A repetition

Leather-bound
Stilled motions
Scratches recalled

Memory
Wounds

Cleaned
Then
I remember her
White nurse's
Uniform
White sneakers

But still a

murmur
I think of death
Plying years
In time

Elevator stops
I hear her
Voice

My thoughts

Lean into my
Wishes

How a return
Makes sense

Blind your mind

There's a voice
My eyes
In stillness
See her
Eyes
Or was that a
Mistaken word

Her breath
On me
She says
Touch my

Mind's

Emotions

Yours
My mind's eye
My hands
Calculate

                                        Take off
                        Your
                        Uniform

Put it on that chair

But she says

It will crash
I repeat
I return
Eyes will
Tell

I'm sure
Pillows remember
Wishes

Your white breasts

Your blue
Eyes

Keep

On seeing

Don't forget it's all
In the mind's body
Please
Push up
My pillows

Take off
Your white uniform

I remember
Catullus riding
My memory

                              Please

Take care
Of
Your senses
And
Then he said
Your uniform

                                              A bath

He wrote
Wash your
Ass

Your hair
Yours truly,
Your

Keep your
Skin perfumed
Your hands
Your velvet hands

In a poem
You shifted my

Dreams
Sequestered

A body poem

Did you know
So much of
You
Rests
In my mind's hands

Your right
Or would you prefer
Your left
She holds a
Needle

A team of first year
Hold
Your future

A needle punctures

Your arm

In a void
Sneakers walk

A doctor

Smiles
Others
imitate

                              A nurse
                              Raises his
                              Pillows

He looks at her
Others wish they
Could do
The same

A smattering
Of death

Her body

Of Joy

Wheels of memory

Dreams of a
Poem pounding
Its wish

Thinks of Foucault
The Use of Pleasure
Or Sade's
Crimes of Love
A rebirth
A nurse's hands
A needle

A desire

Flexing
Her eyes

A desire
In a warrior's hand

Writing
Desire
In a second edition

Check
She
Says
How
About

She moves to his left arm
I'm against it
All The
Same

There's no
Now
Now
Now

Dreams
Easy

Come and
Go

Bed 26
Yells
That
Smell
Of
Soup

A stink
A grin

Doctor
She says

As she whispers

I've
Heard A cat meou
Before

Tonight
A Friday
Prayer

At night
Prayers

    Eat

In the kitchen   Tonight
                                  A round of
                                  Prayers

She says
Same thing
Prayers you've never

                Forgotten
A dinner
You've never
Forgotten

Pull your
White
Blouse
Closer

Further

Down
He hears

The religious Life
Dreams of a man
Bed 26 yells
Do you now

Say at dawn
A branch
Nearly killed
You

She adds softly
She closes the
Curtains
Remembers

So

Many

                                        Others

She pulls
The curtains
To the
Left side

He dreams of
Timothy of
Athens
A bit more
He says
Pull
The curtain
        Down
He says
I can
Only
Dream

                                        Then
                                        It's all

He pushes the curtain
Down his
Dreams

Weeps

Please
Call
A nurse
My tray stinks

Bed 26 yells out
Nurse
He pissed
He smells

Sorry, he says
Sorry
It's
True

Memory adds
It's true
Really
True

                              Weeps old age
                              Change his

Diapers

He read

Part one
His nurse pulls
His sheet
Down

                              A time for mem-

ories

                                    Remembrances

                              Jews
                              Spinoza

                              Eleazar

Any other

Things
You want
To remember?

Words
Faces
Words
Nurse smiles
Remembers
Her mother's Silence

A memory leaps out of her heart

He hears
The elevator

Stop

Somebody   screams
An absence
disappears

Music and then music

Elevator door
Closes
But it knows
Where to go
OK!
Where

                              Close
                              Your
                              Eyes

She says if
You need
Me
In your hand

Call me

Close
Your eyes

He can hear
Corn Flakes
Milk
Corn Flakes

Bed
26
She says
Whispers to herself
Thinks smiling
Shut the
Fuck
Up

OK
A needle prick
Left Leg

Was
The
Coffee
Hot
Enough
She asks
Always Plurals

What's he doing
Now
His needle
He mumbles
Yours truly,
Yours truly
White

All

                              Your

Body

Remembered

Mine all alone
When I hear
Your bag
Yours truly,
Needle smells
Perfume of
Power

All your walk to my
Bed

She whispers
Death
In my
Hand
Your breath

She says
Later
A soft

Sleep

Later
A dream

A white bed
A Whisper
A Shot

He smiles
Then
He whispers
Xmas gift

Mine
Alone
I can sleep
I threw a dream over

The white
Sheet

I think

Whisper
Touches me

She walks around
My bed
Pulls up
My sheet
My pillow

Bed 26 screams
Take care
Of me
My
Shot

He yells
Tell me
How
Long
This curtain

Tell me about Elijah Montalto

or
The Ben Israel
The Naso family

So many other Jews   Judah and Isaac

I
In my memory   I can Tell you
more
Filled with Songs

In Brooklyn
Surrounded by
Friends who opened
A deli
Marx and Engels

Traces
Every where
Your
Well
Memories in Spanish
On Hester

Close to a temple

Hush Hush
She says
She repeats

Now
My memory rests

Hears

Water   A Hush Hush
Running out
Candles in the Living room

Water
I think
Juliet in water

But then
Why not
Cressida
Juliet
Lady Macbeth

                              LUCRECIUS

REMEMBERS
Gertrude Stein
O miracle Painter

Picasso
As quiet
As a front-line speech

                                        A front line

The nurse
Says dream
In
Paris
My great-grand says
Learn a skill

Mommy asks why

Simple!
In a Siberian salt mine
Buddy to my left says
Be careful

Salt
Above
Hammer
In your left
Hand

So
My
Grandfather reminds
Me
In my crib
Watch out!
When will he see
A man
Without
Fingers
He'll say
Reminds
ME

Then off
To Geneva
My mother says

She sat on Lenin's knee
The Left one
The train slowed
Down
At Finland
Station

                                    Later
                                    I say
                                    OK. Then

How will

                                    I Pick
                                    My nose

My grand-father
I say to his memory
Alors
Homme
When you get to
Paris check out
My cemetery
I should be with
All your

FRIENDS
Speaking
Russian

                                        Fine with
                                        Me

Then
I would have said
To his father
The famous rabbi

                                        He did did
                                        Do Lots of

Things
Like? Created

A girls' school
All
You have
To

Do is ask

But I   Don't read
But your hands
As quiet
As a   WWI hole

Nurse
Says
Quiet
Time for   Sleep
                                 Waits

A side of words
Parents
You
Are
My
Angel of pleasures
She hears

She thinks
You're not

See you
Later
Bed 24

And Please
Do Not
Touch
ME
    Front
    Or
    Back

See you
Before
Sunset

A pack of words
In the mind's cubicle
All
In
There

But I truly

Have

To

Imagine

The

Rest

                              My great grandfa-

ther

You

Could

Still hear

His prayers

He knows you

Can't change

A word

So it is written

In Hebrew

Isn't always a

                    Question of

Words?

I promise
I'll not
Call on your
Hear
My Phone

Not
Once

A dream
Late
In a dream

But
Please

                                        Lift

Your shushing mouth

He says to his dream

Meet you
In the dining
Room

There
You can
Take my
Pulse
See. I say
I'm still
Thinking
My hands
On you

Her
Tray
Falls
To the
Floor

Downstairs
I know
She says

There's
Nobody
There

SO THERE those
Who saith
Words
Are always
There in
Their Undeniableness

A voice says

                                        Let there

be

                                        Letters

Alone in
Hebrew
Junior
Puts his
Violin down

His
Scores

I say tomato
You say
Tomatos

Let all things
Be
So saith the
Text
With sacred words

Here
See
A Mouth
Going
As it returns to the
Text mumbles
Discontentment
OK! I hear

The word

Painted
In a violin sound
A violin
Pasted over his
Wrath

Here
Words are
Parcelled

Parodied

Close to
Meaning

                              He says
                              Leave that
                              Bible

Can't

                    You

An

Example
stairs

Paul is up-

Playing
For a 13th year
Old after
Well...you know

Can you
Hear his words
Words away
Dancing
No!
I can
Only
Hear what's to be
Heard mid-morning
Great whatever

Whatever
I don't hear

I can see
Notes
Street Signs

Words paroled

Another   One
Hears
The Unheard

A soundless
Bike
The wind
Wounds
Holds
A lover
His bike gone

He believes
Sneakers
Can be heard

On a silent hope

Only a sound
Corridor
Soundless
White
Sneakers

Hug a
Silence
Dressed in
White

She
Stares
Out
His
Window

Trees sing
Leaves
Fly
Land on a car

Before
He asks
It's my
Shift she says
My rounds
Yours truly,
Left turn
Please…

The sound of
Branches

He dreams
Is she
Clean
Why
He says
As clean
As a
Whistle

He says
Good to
See you
Now
And he adds as in a
Fiction
How was your dinner?

You're my house
Of cards

She says in an accented
India English
Better
Than a House
Of Indian cards

Bed 26 says
The Old Torah
How
About learning how
To forget

                                        "Ouch!"

My pulse
Don't forget

I'd like
With your
Permission
Watch out
Beer
He smiles

                    She says

No beer!

                                        A Bud-

dhist tradition

                                    She mut-

ters

Bed 26 says
Don't forget
His asshole deliveries

He adds
Don't
Pull
Your Blouse
Down

She says
Read me
The Second
Part of
King James
The Second Part
Yes
I say to you
The third
Part

                                 And the
                                 Triadic

And…she says
Don't
Forget   Titus An-

dronicus
Oxford U Press

Don't forget
While we're on it
Timothy of Athens

Nurse, would you
Be kind enough
Pull the shade down

See you
Later
Good Night

How many more
She whispers says
He dribbles a thought

Piss

I'll be right
There!

                              Her

Voice is
An exclamation
He says to himself

There there are
The wives of
Windows

                    The Merry …she

Adds
Now
She remembers
The ground floor dining
Room
Hope she whispers
I'll not be late
At all on my dark shift

Here
No reply

Soundless sneakers

Of memory

                              Mon Coeur avait
                              Raison

Thoughts come
And Go their
Ways

She says
Let me
Wash
Your hands   Your
                                 Hands

He's clean now
She says to the doctor
You
Can
Touch him
My ass
My dreams

I'm
All clean
She whispers
Doc
Why don't you go
To Ines free ?

There's music now
Elevator
Music and Music

Yours truly, This time!
It's all yours
See you downstairs
She whispers
Downstairs
All is ok! on p. 902
She sees herself
Afloat
You knew her
Horatio
You can hear

The lover's heavy
Breathing

He says so much crying
Lay her on
The ground he says

The nurse prepares
Her needle
In hand
She sighs
How
Will sleep
Sleep ever come

A great storm

Leaves
Pile up

Knock! Knock
Whose

There, she asks

I'll be
Right

                                      There in bed

She strains out
Her white
Uniform

See you
Bed 26!

Dumb music
Turn on that dumb light

                    Doctor says

I agree for
Music!   Would
Horatio agree

                             In the

Light of

                             Time out

Got it? Good!

Bed 26 says to the Nurse please give this book
to Number next to mine
Tell him turn to page 78-79. He's a gt biker on
the cover. Tell him I know.

P 78. Thy breasts and hair
        and skin velvet thighs
        are clearer

 P 79. and it flows to and from When will it
        be   me making love that sprang
        From Thee to me—

Wheels turn
I said to myself
Tell her
I'm waiting

                                    I will

Rebirth
As an animal
In your hand

Impartial
A desire of
Love

I know You decypher
My thoughts

Tell 26 many great thanks
Then
She pushes my pillow
A pillow filled with
Desires
Dreams
Say
What will
Happen then

A radio blares

A paperback
Stumbles

I dreamed she had
Stumbled over
Her body

The dirt
The earth
I cry
What will
Happen next

                                        A

HOSPITAL

                                        Leaves
                                        A tree
                                        A

Sound
Dreams come to me
How could I have
Stopped her
When lights

Stay bright

Where have they
All gone?

Desires for her body
Still holding my desires
In
Her left hand

She walks
Still I can hear
Her
Past my Desires

                              Can I

Dream
Of her
Desires

Ok!
She can

Could I barge
Into her desires
In a dream we
Meet under
A fallen tree
Her body in blood

As clean as my
Desires

Her clean Body
Still smelling
Of my

dreams
Out of

A novel

Out of
Her body's
Desires
I've invented

Stop wallowing

On my
Body

                                        Skip my absence

Desires anchored
In my dreams
        Anchored
In half light
I can still breathe
Her body

Is there a wait
A pause
Where
She asks
Where
Are my
Dreams
Dreamt

In my body's
Desires
Like an animal
Waiting

My life beneath
My life

A breach of
Truth

The Emergence

Of truth
Counting
She asks
Where is the
Truth
In a book
Waits
A tombstone
Waits

For desires to flower
In a hand wet with
Desires for a truth

I've waited
As long
As I can
Wait

My nurse
Sneakers in
Says
I'll see
You soon
My needle
Aimed at   your
Left thigh

Clean
Smelling of
Soap
Waiting
Soup
Still   Once
A time

Waiting   A
Dream
The nurse's mouth

Hears itself
By
Itself
Where have they
All gone
She puts
Her needle back

All now gone
It's all a thought
A
Thought

Time for me
Does not stop
Her perfume
Lingers
Above my body

When will
Doc
Let his finger
Roam for dessert

I could have
Sworn

There was another
Balance

I'm still
Wallowing
My desires
A house

Please put my
Legs up

My house of
Bleeding
My memory
Does not forget

Her touching me

Bed 26 has been
Wheeled away
Away dead away
Elevator door glides
Away

Nobody knows
Where he's gone
Must have been
Where I'll be going

Outside
A spiral of thoughts
The nurse hears
Thinking
Will they wait
All of them
Where
Are those
Wheels now
Going

Ask my nurse
Where have my
Wheels
My wheels
All Gone
Downstairs
Gone.

Take a good guess
Where have all my
Wheels gone

                              I should
                              Have shot
                              Those

Branches
Where have all
My buddies
Gone

His voice trails away

Where have they all
Gone
Where
Where have they
Gone

His hands
There are so many
Hands
Fallen off my bed
My nurse
Becomes

      My muse

Serge Gavronsky

SERGE GAVRONSKY, born in Paris, now lives in New York. He was educated at Columbia University, from where he received his Phd in European History. He subsequently held the position of Professor of French Literature and Poetics, at Barnard College, Columbia University. He has published eleven books of poetry in French and in English, in addition to over twenty artist's books in France. In English, he published poetry, fiction and literary criticism, as well as five books of translation of contemporary French poets: *Poems And Texts, The Power Of Language, Toward A New Poetics, Six Contemporary French Women Poets, The Writing Of Appollinaire.* His main focus was the poetry/poetics of Francis Ponge. His more recent publications include: *Silence Of Memory, Truth Truth Truth, Murderous Fantasies,* and *What's The Title? Title.* Louis Zukofsky's "A", co-translated with Francois Dominique, was published in 2020. He is presently writing a new work of poetic fiction.